First Facts™

Holidays and Culture

Day of the Dead

A Celebration of Life and Death

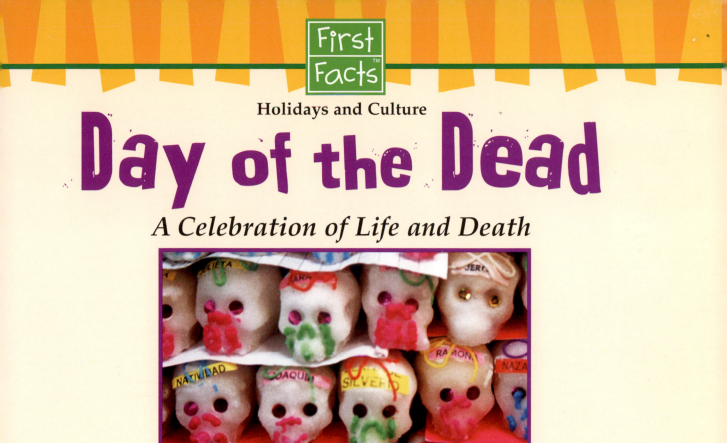

by Amanda Doering

Consultant:
Colin M. MacLachlan
John Christy Barr Distinguished Professor of History
Tulane University
New Orleans, Louisiana

Capstone press

Mankato, Minnesota

First Facts is published by Capstone Press,
151 Good Counsel Drive, P.O. Box 669, Mankato, Minnesota 56002.
www.capstonepress.com

Library of Congress Cataloging-in-Publication Data
Doering, Amanda.
Day of the Dead : a celebration of life and death / by Amanda Doering.
    p. cm.—(First facts. Holidays and culture)
    Summary: "A brief description of what Day of the Dead is, how it started, and ways people
celebrate this cultural holiday"—Provided by publisher.
    Includes bibliographical references and index.
    ISBN-13: 978-0-7368-5388-0 (hardcover)
    ISBN-10: 0-7368-5388-X (hardcover)
    1. All Souls' Day—Mexico—Juvenile literature. 2. Mexico—Social life and customs—Juvenile
literature. 3. Mexico—Religious life and customs—Juvenile literature. I. Title. II. Series.
GT4995.A4D64 2006
394.264'0972—dc22   2005015588

Editorial Credits
Jennifer Besel, editor; Juliette Peters, designer; Wanda Winch, photo researcher; Scott Thoms,
    photo editor

Photo Credits
AP Photo/Eduardo Verdugo, 20; Art Directors/E. James, 14; Aurora/Russell Gordon, 11, 15;
Capstone Press/Karon Dubke, 21; Corbis/Anders Ryman, 19; The Granger Collection, New
York, 9; The Image Works/Jack Kurtz, 4–5; Iraq war altar created by Olvera Street artists:
Ginette Rondeau, Juliane Backmann, Al Herian, Gabriela Quintero, Bonjunnie Comostiles/photo
by Juliane Backmann, 12–13; North Wind Picture Archives, 8; Photo courtesy of Olvera Street
artist Ginette Rondeau, 17; SuperStock/age fotostock, cover; Woodfin Camp & Associates
Inc./Robert Frerck, 1, 6–7, 16

1 2 3 4 5 6 11 10 09 08 07 06

Table of Contents

Celebrating Day of the Dead

In the flickering candlelight, a Mexican family prays for the **spirits** of relatives. They smile as they remember stories about loved ones who have died. The family is celebrating Day of the Dead.

Fact!
Some families have mariachi bands play music at the cemetery.

What Is Day of the Dead?

Each year on November 1 and 2, Mexican families celebrate Day of the Dead. This holiday is a time to remember people who have died.

Day of the Dead isn't a scary holiday. In Mexican **culture**, death is a part of life. **Customs** of the holiday help families honor the dead.

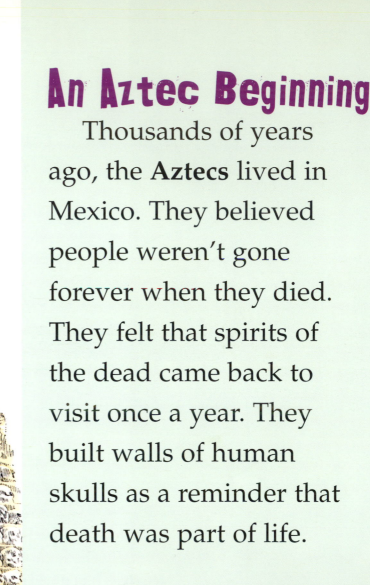

An Aztec Beginning

Thousands of years ago, the **Aztecs** lived in Mexico. They believed people weren't gone forever when they died. They felt that spirits of the dead came back to visit once a year. They built walls of human skulls as a reminder that death was part of life.

Spanish settlers came to Mexico in
the 1500s. They wanted the Aztecs to
be **Christians**. But the Aztecs wanted to
keep their own traditions.

Preparing the Altar

Today, Day of the Dead is a mix of Christian and Aztec customs. Many Mexicans still believe spirits of the dead come back once a year.

To welcome the spirits home, families build **altars**. Candles, food, and flowers decorate tables and shelves. Pictures of loved ones and Christian saints are proudly displayed among the decorations.

Fact!

Day of the Dead is celebrated at the same time as the Christian holiday All Saints' Day.

Mexican Americans

Many people think Day of the Dead is the Mexican Halloween, but that is not true. This holiday is a special time to honor people who have died.

In some communities, Mexican Americans build altars on sidewalks, so everyone can share this Mexican tradition. Many of the altars honor American soldiers or people who died in accidents.

Visiting the Cemetery

Day of the Dead is a time for families to visit cemeteries. They wash and decorate their relatives' gravestones. Marigold flowers are laid out to lead the spirits home.

Many families stay in the cemeteries all day and night. They sing, eat, and pray to honor the lives of their loved ones.

Skulls and Skeletons

In Mexico, skulls and skeletons stand for life and death. Shops sell candy skulls made of sugar. These fun candies remind people that death isn't a scary part of life.

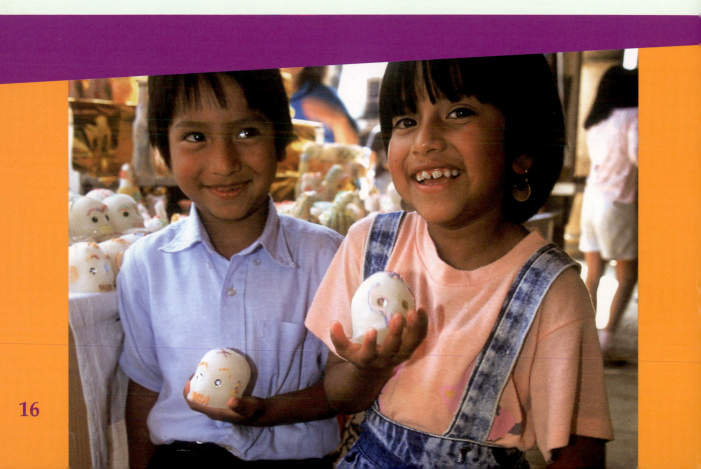

On Day of the Dead, skeletons are often seen walking down streets. That's because adults, and even children, wear skeleton costumes in parades.

Food

No one wants the spirits to be hungry, so lots of food is made for Day of the Dead. Families make foods their loved ones liked. Some of the food is left out as **offerings** at cemeteries or on altars.

Remembering the dead is an important part of the Mexican way of life. Day of the Dead is a true celebration of people, history, and culture.

Amazing Holiday Story!

Day of the Dead is a time to honor all people who have died. In 2004, as part of a Day of the Dead celebration, people from the United States and Mexico met at the border between the two countries. Together, they celebrated Day of the Dead by honoring those who died trying to immigrate to the United States.

Hands On: Paper Flowers

Mexican children often make paper flowers to put on the altars or graves of their relatives. You can make a paper flower for someone you care about.

What You Need

4 sheets of colored tissue paper
  (6 inches by 12 inches or
  15 centimeters by 30 centimeters)
scissors
1 green pipe cleaner

What You Do

1. Stack the four sheets of paper on top of each other.
2. Fold the length of the stack of papers in 1 inch (2.5 centimeters) from the edge. Continue by fan-folding the paper.
3. Cut the folded paper at both ends, rounding the corners.
4. Fold the pipe cleaner in half around the middle of the paper. Twist the pipe cleaner tightly around the paper.
5. Fan out the layers of paper on both sides of the pipe cleaner. Be careful not to tear the paper. Arrange the paper to look like flower petals.
6. Shape one end of the pipe cleaner to look like a leaf.

Glossary

altar (AWL-tur)—a table used for ceremonies or rituals

Aztecs (AZ-teks)—Indian people who lived in Mexico before Spanish people settled there

Christian (KRISS-chin)—a person who follows a religion based on the teachings of Jesus Christ

culture (KUHL-chur)—a people's way of life, ideas, art, customs, and traditions

custom (KUHSS-tuhm)—a tradition in a culture or society

offering (OF-ur-ing)—a gift or contribution

spirit (SPIHR-it)—the part of a person that is believed to control thoughts and feelings; the spirit is also called the soul.

Read More

Gnojewski, Carol. *Day of the Dead: A Latino Celebration of Family and Life.* Finding Out About Holidays. Berkeley Heights, N.J.: Enslow, 2005.

Lowery, Linda. *Day of the Dead.* On My Own Holidays. Minneapolis: Carolrhoda Books, 2004.

Internet Sites

FactHound offers a safe, fun way to find Internet sites related to this book. All of the sites on FactHound have been researched by our staff.

Here's how:
1. Visit *www.facthound.com*
2. Type in this special code **073685388X** for age-appropriate sites. Or enter a search word related to this book for a more general search.
3. Click on the **Fetch It** button.

FactHound will fetch the best sites for you!

Index